STARS OF SPORTS

DIANA TAURASI

HOOPS LEGEND

by Shane Frederick

CAPSTONE PRESS
a capstone imprint

Stars of Sports is published by Capstone Press, an imprint of Capstone.
1710 Roe Crest Drive, North Mankato, Minnesota 56003
www.capstonepub.com

**Library of Congress Cataloging-in-Publication Data is available on the Library of
Congress website.**
ISBN: 978-1-4966-8384-7 (hardcover)
ISBN: 978-1-4966-8435-6 (eBook PDF)

Summary: As a child, Diana Taurasi was tall and gangly. But as soon as she started
playing basketball, she learned that her size and height gave her an advantage on the
basketball court. Taurasi has come a long way since then. Discover more about her
highlights on and off the court.

Editorial Credits
Editor: Anna Butzer; Designer: Sarah Bennett; Media Researcher: Eric Gohl;
Production Specialist: Laura Manthe

Image Credits
Associated Press: Bill Kostroun, 19, Kamil Krzaczynski, 5, Will Powers, 21;
Dreamstime: Jerry Coli, 9, Michele Morrone, 28; Getty Images: Al Schaben, 11, Elsa,
7; Newscom: Icon Sportswire/Mingo Nesmith, cover, Reuters/Rick Scuteri, 22, 23;
Shutterstock: EFKS, 1; Sports Illustrated: Bill Frakes, 14, Bob Rosato, 25, Damian
Strohmeyer, 12, Erick W. Rasco, 27, John W. McDonough, 24, Manny Millan, 13, 16,
Robert Beck, 26

Direct Quotations
Page 17, "The best way to . . ." Daily Collegian, "UConn's Taurasi Proves Why She's Best
in Nation," March 30, 2004, https://www.collegian.psu.edu/archives/article_f20559d9-
a0f7-51af-97d0-304c050476b5.html
Accessed on March 13, 2020.

Printed in the United States of America.
PA117

TABLE OF CONTENTS

Glossary terms are **BOLD** on first use.

CLUTCH PLAYER

Diana Taurasi was struggling. She was missing shots. She was making **turnovers**. Her team was losing.

It was Game 3 of the 2014 Women's National Basketball Association (WNBA) Finals. The Phoenix Mercury trailed the Chicago Sky at the start of the fourth quarter. Taurasi had scored 10 points, but none in the third quarter. One of her best teammates was on the bench with an injury.

But something changed in the final quarter. Taurasi took over. Her shots started going in. She swished one three-pointer and made another with a **bank shot**. She made five baskets and missed only one shot. Taurasi scored 14 points in the quarter, and the Mercury won 87–82 to clinch the championship.

Taurasi won her second WNBA championship and was named the Finals' Most Valuable Player (MVP) for the second time in her career.

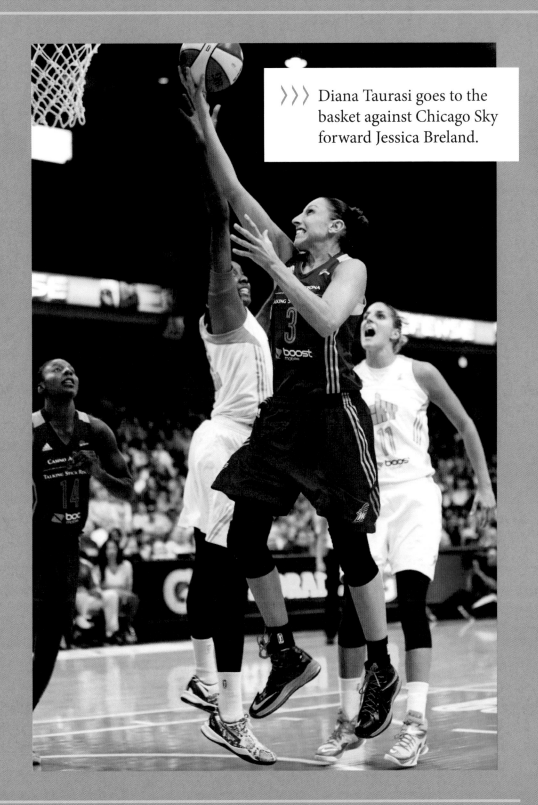

>>> Diana Taurasi goes to the basket against Chicago Sky forward Jessica Breland.

CHAPTER ONE

HIGH SCHOOL STAR

Diana Taurasi was born on June, 11, 1982, in Glendale, California. She grew up in Chino, California, not far from the big city of Los Angeles.

Diana's mother, Lily, was from Argentina. Her father, Mario, was born in Italy but moved to Argentina as a young boy. The couple moved to the United States not long before Diana, their second daughter, was born.

FACT

The first language Diana Taurasi learned to speak was Spanish.

>>> Taurasi celebrates a win with her father.

BASKETBALL CRAZY

The Taurasis encouraged Diana and her sister, Jessika, to play sports. Diana soon became crazy about basketball. She learned everything she could about the sport. Her idol was Earvin "Magic" Johnson, the great player for the Los Angeles Lakers of the National Basketball Association (NBA).

Magic could do everything on a basketball court. He scored lots of points, but he was also one of the best ball handlers and passers of all time. Diana studied Magic's moves and tried to copy them when she was playing.

Diana almost always had a basketball with her. She dribbled it everywhere she went. She would dribble it from home to the playground for a game and back home again. She even dribbled inside the house—at least until her mom told her to stop.

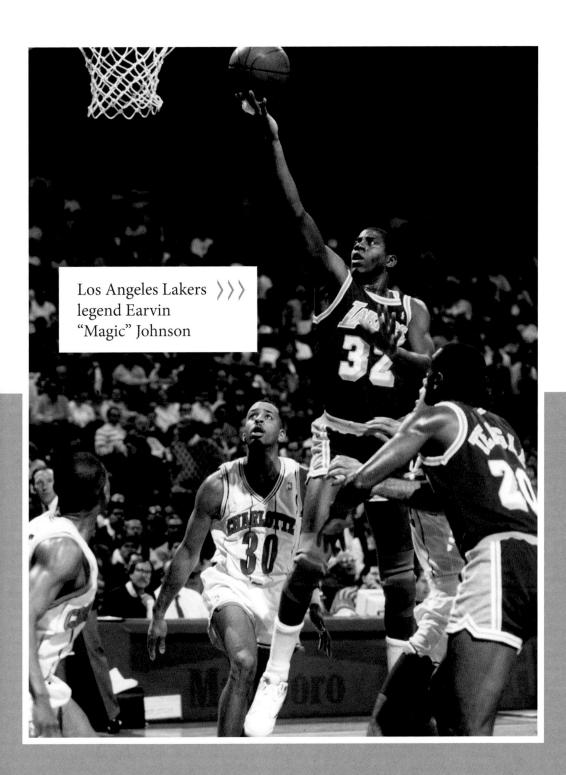

Los Angeles Lakers
legend Earvin
"Magic" Johnson 〉〉〉

RISING STAR

Two years later, before she was even in high school, college teams began recruiting her.

Diana played high school basketball as a ninth-grader at Don Lugo High School in Chino. She **dominated** games. She scored over 50 points in a game several times. That included a 56-point performance during her junior season. As a senior, Diana **averaged** 28.8 points, 12.9 **rebounds**, and 4.2 **assists** per game.

In 2000, after her final season, she was named the top high school girls basketball player in the country. Colleges from all over the country wanted Diana Taurasi to play for them.

⟨⟨⟨ Taurasi battles for a loose
ball during a game in 2000.

CHAPTER TWO

UCONN GOLD

Taurasi had a tough decision to make. She could play basketball for any college in the country. Lily hoped her daughter would stay close to home in southern California. Her dad was impressed by University of Connecticut coach Geno Auriemma. Auriemma, like Mario, was born in Italy. More importantly, Auriemma had one of the best teams in the country. The UConn Huskies had won national championships in 1995 and 2000.

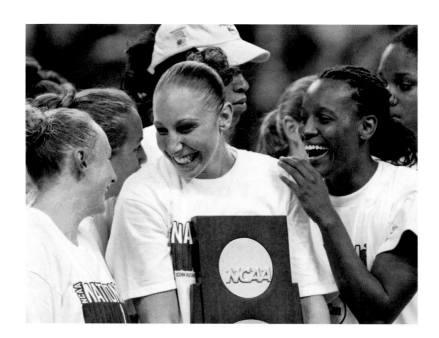

‹‹‹ Taurasi (3) in action against opponents from the University of Tennessee.

Taurasi decided to go across the country to play for UConn. The Huskies had great players, including Sue Bird. Taurasi came off the bench during most of her first season. She moved into a starting role when other players were lost because of injuries.

The Huskies hoped to win a second straight National Collegiate Athletic Association (NCAA) title that year. They made it all the way to the Final Four but lost in the national semifinals. Taurasi made sure that would never happen again while she was there.

The next season, the Huskies didn't lose a single game. They had a record of 39–0 and won the national championship.

At 6 feet (183 cm) tall, Taurasi was part of a powerhouse lineup that included Bird, Swin Cash, Asjha Jones, and Tamika Williams. Taurasi showed off her greatness during a regular-season game against the number-two ranked Tennessee Volunteers. She scored 32 points and helped lead UConn to a big win.

〉〉〉 Taurasi goes up against Stacey Dales of Oklahoma in the NCAA Finals in 2002.

During the NCAA **tournament**, the Huskies defeated Tennessee in the semifinals and Oklahoma in the championship game to cap off the perfect season.

Taurasi was the only starter to return to the team in 2002–03. She didn't let that phase her, and the Huskies were just as good. They lost only one game that season and won their second straight title. Taurasi scored 28 points in the championship game against Tennessee. She was named the tournament's most outstanding player and won the Naismith Award as the best player in women's college basketball.

FACT

The Naismith Award is named after the inventor of basketball, James Naismith. It is given annually to the most outstanding male player and female player.

CAN'T STOP CONNECTICUT

Connecticut had a record of 31–4 during Taurasi's final season there. She finished off her career on top as the Huskies won a third-straight national championship. Once again they defeated **rival** Tennessee in the final game. Taurasi scored 17 points in the final and was again named the tournament's top player.

>>> The Huskies celebrate after winning the 2004 NCAA Finals.

When asked before the tournament why his team would win another championship, coach Auriemma said, "The best way to explain it is that we have Diana and you don't. And every other team in this tournament wishes they had her."

At the end of her senior season, Taurasi won the Naismith Award again. During Taurasi's time at Connecticut, the Huskies won 139 games and lost only eight times. Doing everything well like her hero Magic Johnson, she became the first player in the school's history to score 2,000 points, dish out 600 assists, and grab 600 rebounds.

The Streak

During Taurasi's sophomore and junior seasons at UConn, the Huskies won 70 games in a row. That streak included a 39–0 record during her sophomore season and wins in the first 31 games of her junior year. The Huskies went 139–8 during her time at UConn.

CHAPTER THREE

ON TO THE PROS

The Phoenix Mercury had the first overall pick in the 2004 WNBA **draft**. There was only one choice. The Mercury knew Diana Taurasi could turn around their troubled franchise.

Taurasi joined the Mercury shortly after her college career ended. She became a starter and an instant star.

Taurasi scored 22 points in her very first **professional** game. She then became the first player in WNBA history to score 20 points or more in each of her first three games. That first season, she led the Mercury to nine more wins than they had the year before. She averaged 17 points per game that season and was named WNBA **Rookie** of the Year and First Team All-WNBA.

WNBA President Val Ackerman poses with Taurasi ⟩⟩⟩ after she was drafted by the Phoenix Mercury.

OUT OF THIS WORLD

With Taurasi leading the way, the Mercury knew they could one day land a WNBA championship. It took a few years, but Phoenix eventually found its way to the top of the league.

Taurasi played in her first WNBA All-Star Game in 2005. She went again in 2006. That season she averaged a career high of 25.3 points per game. During one game that year, she set a league record by scoring 47 points in a 111–110 triple-overtime victory over the Houston Comets.

The 2007 season was Taurasi's fourth season in the league. She continued her stellar play, scoring an average of 19.2 points per game. The Mercury became one of the best teams in the league. Phoenix went 23–11. The season before Taurasi arrived, they were 8–26.

<<< Taurasi shoots over an opponent from the Houston Comets.

Call her "Dee"

Diana Taurasi has many nicknames, including "D.T." and "Dee." Some have come from friends, some have come from admirers. One admirer was Kobe Bryant. He was known as the "Black Mamba" when he played for the Los Angeles Lakers because of his killer instinct similar to the dangerous snake. He called Taurasi "White Mamba."

During the 2007 WNBA playoffs, the Mercury swept the Seattle Storm and the San Antonio Silver Stars in the first two rounds. That set up a meeting with the Detroit Shock in the WNBA Finals.

The Mercury and Shock each won two games. It came down to Game 5 to decide the champion. Taurasi scored 17 points, grabbed seven rebounds, and passed out six assists. The game ended at 108–92, and the Mercury had won their first championship.

⟨⟨⟨ Taurasi drives past Detroit Shock opponents during the WNBA Finals in 2007.

Two seasons later, Taurasi and the Mercury won another championship. They defeated the Indiana Fever 3–2 in the Finals. Taurasi scored 26 points in Game 5 to lead the way to the title. After the season Taurasi was named WNBA MVP.

Phoenix won a third title in 2014. Taurasi averaged 20.3 points per game in the three-game sweep over the Chicago Sky.

FACT

In 2017, Taurasi became the WNBA's all-time leading scorer. Through the 2019 season, she had 8,575 points.

CHAPTER FOUR
GOOD AS GOLD

Taurasi had a fun year in 2004. She won a third straight championship at UConn. She became a professional basketball player. She also became an Olympian for the first time.

Taurasi traveled to Athens, Greece, to play for Team USA. She wasn't a starter, but she came off the bench and averaged 8.8 points per game. The U.S. won the gold medal, defeating Australia in the final.

⟩⟩⟩ Team USA poses after winning the gold medal at the 2004 Summer Olympics in Athens, Greece.

Taurasi in action during a game against Russia in the 2008 Summer Olympics in Beijing, China.

Four years later, in 2008, Taurasi was on the U.S. Olympic team again. Her coach was someone she knew very well, her old college coach, Geno Auriemma. That year in Beijing, China, Taurasi was a starter. She averaged 19.5 points over eight games. The U.S. defeated Australia again for the gold medal.

GOLD NEVER GETS OLD

Taurasi continued to collect gold medals. Playing for Coach Auriemma again she won two more Olympic championships. In 2012, in London, England, she averaged 20 points per game on her way to a third gold medal. The U.S. outscored Australia once again. In 2016, in Rio de Janeiro, Brazil, she averaged 25.8 points per game, and Team USA beat Spain in the final game.

Taurasi (12) goes up for a shot during the 2012 Summer Olympics. 〉〉〉

<<< Taurasi (second from left) celebrates another win with her teammates after the 2016 Summer Olympics in Rio de Janeiro, Brazil.

Taurasi is one of only five athletes in history who has four Olympic gold medals in basketball. Nobody has five. Taurasi also has represented the United States in world championships and has been named USA Basketball's female player of the year four times.

FACT

Taurasi is one of only 11 players to have earned an Olympic gold medal, a world championship, an NCAA championship, and a WNBA title.

STILL GOING STRONG

Diana Taurasi has been one of the best basketball players in the world for many years. She won four straight WNBA scoring titles. She was a nine-time All-Star and a 10-time All-WNBA pick. After 15 seasons in the WNBA, her playing career will soon be over. But it's not done yet.

Because of injuries, she played in only six games during the 2019 WNBA season. After the season ended she worked hard to recover and get herself in shape for 2020. That year wouldn't just be her 16th pro season. It would be another Olympic year and a chance to win a fifth gold medal.

〉〉〉 Taurasi looks for an opening in a game against Latvia's women's national team.

TIMELINE

1982 Born in Glendale, California

2000 Named the top high school girls basketball player in the country

2001 Begins playing for University of Connecticut

2003 Wins the Naismith Award as best player in women's college basketball

2004 The Phoenix Mercury drafts Diana as their first pick

2004 Wins WNBA Rookie of the Year

2005 Plays in first WNBA All-Star Game

2009 Named WNBA MVP

2016 Wins her fourth Olympic gold medal with Team USA

2018 Becomes first player in WNBA history to reach 8,000 career points

GLOSSARY

ASSIST (uh-SIST)—a pass that leads to a score by a teammate

AVERAGE (AV-uh-rij)—a player's total points, blocks, or rebounds in a season divided by the number of games played

BANK SHOT (BANGK SHOT)—a shot in basketball in which the ball hits off the backboard before going into the basket

DOMINATE (DAH-muh-nayt)—to control or rule over

DRAFT (DRAFT)—the process of choosing a person to join a sports organization or team

PROFESSIONAL (pruh-FESH-uh-nuhl)—a level of a sport in which players get paid to play

REBOUND (REE-bound)—catching a ball that has missed the basket

RIVAL (RYE-vuhl)—a person, or team, competing with another for the same thing

ROOKIE (RUK-ee)—a player in his or her first year

TOURNAMENT (TUR-nuh-muhnt)—a series of matches between several players or teams, ending in one winner

TURNOVER (TURN-oh-vur)—when a team loses possession of the ball

READ MORE

Flynn, Brendan. *Superstars of the WNBA Finals*. North Minneapolis: Cody Koala, 2019.

Ignotofsky, Rachel. *Women in Sports: 50 Fearless Athletes Who Played to Win*. Berkeley, CA: Ten Speed Press, 2017.

Omoth, Tyler. *The WNBA Finals*. North Mankato, MN: Capstone Press, 2020.

INTERNET SITES

Diana Taurasi
dianataurasi.com

WNBA
www.wnba.com

WNBA Facts for Kids
kids.kiddle.co/Women%27s_National_Basketball_Association

INDEX